# ARE YOU RELATED ★TO A★ROCK STAR?

# ARE YOU RELATED TO A ROCK STAR?

## A GUIDE TO UNLOCKING YOUR SECRET FAMILY HISTORY

by
Kris Hirschmann

Scholastic Inc.

New York   Toronto   London   Auckland
Sydney   Mexico City   New Delhi   Hong Kong

*For my many loved ones who are gone
but not forgotten.*
*— K.H.*

ISBN 978-0-545-28223-9

12 11 10 9 8 7 6 5 4 3 2 1          11 12 13 14 15 16/0

Printed in the U.S.A.                                40
First Scholastic printing, February 2011

# Contents

## Section 1
## The Basics

**WOULD YOU** like to hear a story? It's an exciting tale that takes place all over the world and stretches into the distant past. It includes heroes, villains, and maybe even a celebrity or two. And best of all, it's about you. Yes, YOU!

Think we're joking? We aren't. You have a family, and your family has a unique history. **You can learn about this history—and this book will show you how to do it.** It'll take a little time and a little work to get the job done. But it's *fun* work. And as millions of people already know, the rewards are worth the effort. So get ready to embark on an amazing journey of discovery. Let's bring a little bit of the **past** . . . into the **present**!

# What Is Genealogy?

Did you know that President Barack Obama is related to former President George W. Bush and former Vice President Dick Cheney? Oh, and he's a distant cousin of actor Brad Pitt, too.

Speaking of distant cousins, it turns out that Britney Spears isn't just a pop princess. She has real royal blood running through her veins. Spears has family ties to Monaco's Prince Albert II. Now *that* would be an interesting family reunion!

And here's another fun fact. Singer Justin Bieber probably had some industrious German ancestors. The surname "Bieber" comes from an old German word for "beaver." In long-ago Germany, this nickname was given to a community's hardest and best workers. So success clearly runs in Bieber's family.

## Ancestor-Speak

An **ancestor** is a person's relative from the distant past.

An ancestor's children, grandchildren, great-grandchildren, and so on are called **descendants**.

## Just the Facts

Facts like these don't start out as common knowledge. Researchers discover them by digging through piles of old

2

records. They learn the names of a person's parents, grandparents, great-grandparents, and other ancestors. At the same time, other researchers are learning about different family lines. Sooner or later, links may pop up.

What exactly is a "link"? A link is any ancestor who appears in two family lines. **Every** descendant of this ancestor shares a blood tie. In other words, these people are related to each other. The study of these relationships is called **genealogy**.

**Get It Right**

It's genealogy with an **a**, not geneology with an **o**. Don't get tripped up by this common spelling mistake.

You don't need any special training to be a genealogist. Anyone can do it—yes, even kids! And the best part is, you can do it **your way**. You can be casual and learn a little, or get serious and learn a lot. Either way, you're guaranteed to have fun. It's like a detective job, but with no pressure, no deadline, and no bad guys. Well, maybe a few outlaws, if you're lucky. (More about this on pages 40 and 41.) This book will explain how *you* can become a family detective!

# More Celebrity Relatives

Some researchers are fascinated by celebrity families. They study their favorite stars to see what interesting facts they can find. Here are a few things genealogists have discovered.

## A "Jolie" Good Time

You already know about Brad Pitt's White House connection. It turns out that Pitt's partner, actress Angelina Jolie, has political ties of her own. She's related to U.S. Secretary of State Hillary Clinton. She's also a distant cousin of Camilla Parker-Bowles, who is married to Prince Charles of the United Kingdom.

## Moving Fast

Like Justin Bieber, pop singer Taylor Swift has a revealing last name. "Swift" is an English surname that means "fast" (duh). One of Taylor's ancestors was probably a speedy British chap!

## Pop Dynasty

Pop stars Madonna, Celine Dion, and Gwen Stefani share more than a love of music. They have common ancestors as well. That's right: These three songbirds are distant cousins.

## Award-Winning Cousins

Since their college days, actors Matt Damon and Ben Affleck have been BFFs. But they're not *just* best buddies. They're related! A bricklayer who died in 1655 was the tenth great-grandfather of both Hollywood stars.

## Well Connected

Former Alaska governor and U.S. vice presidential candidate Sarah Palin has quite a few famous relatives. Palin has family ties to computer mogul Bill Gates, actress Shirley Temple, and actor Alec Baldwin, to name just a few.

## A Web of Relatives

Remember when we mentioned that Monaco's Prince Albert II is related to Britney Spears? Well, that's just the start of it. The man seems to be related to *everyone*. Prince Albert's extended family includes author Laura Ingalls Wilder, scientist Charles Darwin,

### Who Do You Think You Are?

In a popular TV series called *Who Do You Think You Are?* celebrities use genealogical research tools to uncover their past. Versions of the series have aired in seven countries, starting in Great Britain in 2004. The first American season of the show ran in 2010. The premiere episode featured film and stage star Matthew Broderick.

supermodel Cindy Crawford, chef Julia Child, entertainment icon Walt Disney, and dozens of other famous folk.

## Born in the U.S.A.

Singer Bruce Springsteen is famous for his song "Born in the U.S.A." But the rock star's roots are not as all-American as his music. "Springsteen" is a Dutch name, and at least one branch of Bruce's family hails from Ireland.

## President "O'Bama"

Speaking of Ireland, President Barack Obama has a bit o' the green running through his veins. Obama's third great-grandfather, Fulmoth Kearney, emigrated to the United States from Moneygall, Ireland, in 1850.

## Which Witch?

Actress Emma Watson plays a wizard named Hermione Granger in the popular Harry Potter films. It appears that Watson has magic in her real life, too. She is related to Joan Playle, an Englishwoman who was convicted of witchcraft in the 1500s.

## The Ellen Circle

Take a deep breath for this one! According to researchers at the New England Historic Genealogical Society, actor and talk-show host Ellen DeGeneres is part of a unique circle of cousins. Here's how it works:

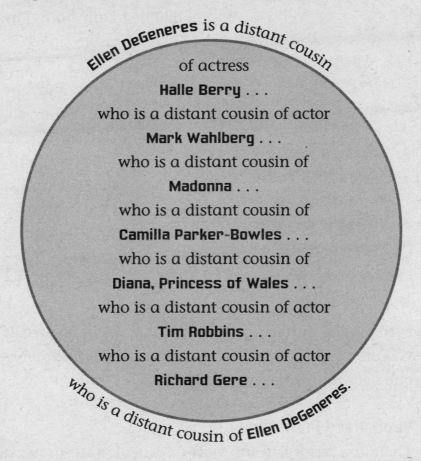

Ellen DeGeneres is a distant cousin of actress
**Halle Berry** . . .
who is a distant cousin of actor
**Mark Wahlberg** . . .
who is a distant cousin of
**Madonna** . . .
who is a distant cousin of
**Camilla Parker-Bowles** . . .
who is a distant cousin of
**Diana, Princess of Wales** . . .
who is a distant cousin of actor
**Tim Robbins** . . .
who is a distant cousin of actor
**Richard Gere** . . .
who is a distant cousin of **Ellen DeGeneres.**

And there you have it! We've come full circle!

# What's in It for Me?

Let's slow down for a sec. On the last few pages, we've been talking about presidents, singers, and actors. Wow, those people are cool and amazing! It's no wonder they have fascinating family histories. Your background is going to be totally boring by comparison, right?

Well, no.

Celebrities may be more famous than you. In genealogical terms, however, they're nothing special. They're just people with families. So President Obama is related to Brad Pitt? That's interesting. But maybe *you're* related to someone even **more intriguing**. In fact, **you probably are**. If you dig deep enough, you're almost sure to find someone notable in your extended family.

### What's the Story?

Actress Sarah Jessica Parker found some interesting family stories when she poked into her past. She discovered one relative who was accused in the Salem witch trials. Another relative had perished in the California gold rush of the mid-1800s.

## Your Place in History

The fame factor is a fun part of genealogy. It draws a lot of people—maybe including **you**—into the hobby.

Pretty soon, though, most genealogists change their focus. They stop looking for celebrity relatives and start looking for stories instead.

What kind of stories are we talking about? Anything, really. You might learn about an ancestor who left his family behind to come to America. You might find out that your relatives fought in the American Civil War—maybe even on both sides! You might discover ancestors who helped settle the Old West. The possibilities are endless.

Stories like these bring history to life. They give people a rush that can only be satisfied by another story, and another, and another. Try it and you'll see. You're about to find your place in history, and genealogy is the map that will show you the way.

**Ancestor-Speak**

An **extended family** is any group of people related by blood, marriage, or both.

# Fourth Cousins Twice Removed . . . Huh?

So you're about to uncover a bunch of cool relatives. That's awesome. But you know what's even **more** awesome? Genealogy doesn't simply show relationships. It also gives you specific terms to define them. So you might say, for instance, "Miley Cyrus is my eleventh cousin twice removed on my mother's side," and any genealogist will know **exactly** what you mean.

## Ancestor-Speak

The prefix "step" identifies an unrelated person who marries one of your biological parents or grandparents, or someone who is descended from that person. An unrelated man who marries your mother, for instance, is your **stepfather**. If your stepmother or stepfather has children, those children are your **stepbrothers** or **stepsisters**.

Take a moment to read the relationship definitions on the next few pages. This information will help you to keep things straight when you start your research.

## The Direct Line

Your mom and dad are your **parents**. Your parents' parents are your **grandparents**. Your grandparents' parents are your **great-grandparents**. Technically they're your *first* great-grandparents, but you can skip the "first." For each generation further back, add the next number in order: **second great-grandparents**, **third great-grandparents**, and so on.

## Sibling Stuff

Your siblings are your **brothers** and **sisters**. Your parents' siblings and their spouses are your **aunts** and **uncles**. Your grandparents' siblings and their spouses are your **great-aunts** and **great-uncles**. For each generation further back, add the next number in order: **second great-aunt**, **third great-uncle**, and so on.

## Closest Cousins

The children of your aunts and uncles are your **first cousins**. Sometimes people just call them "cousins" for short. In genealogy, though, the term "cousin" is not specific—as you're about to see!

## Skipping a Generation

Here's where things start to get tricky. When your first cousins have children, those children are your **first cousins once removed**. (The word "removed" means a skipped generation.) If your first cousins once removed have children, these children are your **first cousins twice removed** because now you've skipped *two* generations. Add the next number in order for succeeding generations: **three times removed, four times removed,** and so on.

## Distant Cousins

Any two people who share a great-grandparent, second great-grandparent, and so on, are distant cousins. The exact definition of the relationship depends on the number of "greats." People with a common *first* great-grandparent are *second* cousins. People with a common *second* great-grandparent are *third* cousins. Add the next number in order for succeeding generations: fourth cousins, fifth cousins, and so on.

Thirty U.S. states ban marriage between first cousins. Six states ban marriage between first cousins once removed.

## Putting It All Together

We have now arrived at the place where genealogy might make your head spin. When you combine distant cousins with skipped generations, you get into the whole "fourth cousin twice removed" thing.

No matter how familiar you are with family charts, it can be hard to figure this stuff out—and many genealogists don't even bother. They just use computer programs to crunch the generational numbers. You can do the same, when the time comes. For now, simply understanding the concept is enough. And aren't you glad to hear that?

## Pop Quiz

**Q:** Say your grandma has just one brother and just one child. What relation to you is your grandma's brother's son's first cousin?

**A:** Your mom or dad.

Confusing? Let's take it step by step: Your grandma's brother is your great-uncle. Your great-uncle's son and your grandma's only child are first cousins. And your grandma's child, of course, is your mom or dad. Ta-da!

## The Basics

## Look It Up

This chart will help you define family relationships. To use the chart,

- choose two relatives. Figure out which ancestor they have in common.

- look at the chart's top row. Find the first person's relationship to the common ancestor. Imagine, for example, that the person is the ancestor's **great-grandchild**.

| | Child | Grandchild | Great-grandchild | |
|---|---|---|---|---|
| **Child** | Sibling | Nephew or niece | Grand-nephew or -niece | |
| **Grandchild** | Nephew or niece | First cousin | Grand-nephew or -niece | |
| **Great-grandchild** | Grand-nephew or -niece | First cousin once removed | Second cousin | |
| **2nd great-grandchild** | Great-grand-nephew or -niece | First cousin twice removed | Second cousin once removed | |
| **3rd great-grandchild** | 2nd great-grand-nephew or -niece | First cousin three times removed | Second cousin twice removed | |
| **4th great-grandchild** | 3rd great-grand-nephew or -niece | First cousin four times removed | Second cousin three times removed | |

- look at the chart's left-hand column. Find the second person's relationship to the common ancestor. Imagine, for example, that the person is the ancestor's **child**.

- find the box where the chosen row and column meet. This box defines the relationship between the two people. In our example, one relative is the **grandnephew or -niece** of the other.

| 2nd great-grandchild | 3rd great-grandchild | 4th great-grandchild |
|---|---|---|
| Great-grand-nephew or -niece | 2nd great-grand-nephew or -niece | 3rd great-grand-nephew or -niece |
| Great-grand-nephew or -niece | 2nd great-grand-nephew or -niece | 3rd great-grand-nephew or -niece |
| Second cousin once removed | Second cousin twice removed | Second cousin three times removed |
| Third cousin | Third cousin once removed | Third cousin twice removed |
| Third cousin once removed | Fourth cousin | Fourth cousin once removed |
| Third cousin twice removed | Fourth cousin once removed | Fifth cousin |

## Trunks, Branches, and Leaves

There's one last thing we need to discuss before you get started. It's the concept of the **family tree**.

A family tree is a chart that organizes your relatives and shows how they connect to each other. Most researchers place themselves at the base of the tree. Earlier generations occupy higher and higher levels.

It's not hard to see where family trees get their name. These charts start with one person. You could call this person the tree's trunk. The trunk rises and splits into two, then four, then eight family branches, or even more. The members of these branches are like the tree's leaves. The more generations you add, the bigger and leafier the tree becomes.

How big is big? It depends. Serious researchers sometimes create **enormous** family trees. A really large tree may have thousands of relatives dangling from its branches. **But don't worry. Your tree doesn't have to be like that.** Start with just yourself plus your parents, grandparents, and great-grandparents for a manageable family tree. You can always add more relatives later, when you're a pro at the whole genealogy thing.

## What's on the Tree?

Family trees include certain standard information and symbols. These things make it easy for genealogists to understand each other's work. This simple tree shows you the basics.

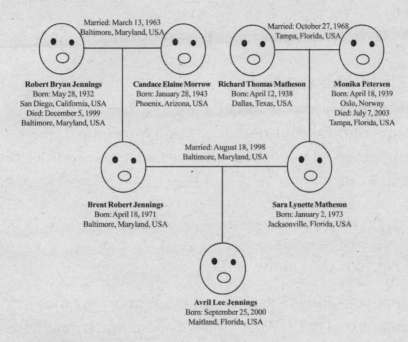

*Name.* Include each person's full name.

*Maiden name.* Women are identified by their maiden names, not their married names.

*Birth.* Include each person's date and place of birth.

*Death.* Include each person's date and place of death (if applicable).

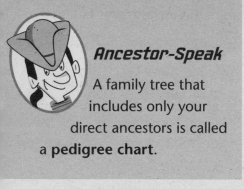

A family tree that includes only your direct ancestors is called a **pedigree chart**.

*Married.* Include each couple's date and place of marriage.

*Horizontal lines* between two people indicate marriage.

*Vertical lines* indicate children born from a marriage.

## Fill in the Blanks

Relationship charts like the one on the opposite page help organize your research. Ask a grown-up to photocopy these pages for you. Use the chart to keep track of your work.

### Hints:

• Put your own name on Line 1.

• Put your father's name on Line 2 and your mother's name on Line 3. Work your way backward from there.

• Males always go on even-numbered lines. Females always go on odd-numbered lines.

• Record marriage dates and places under the man's name.

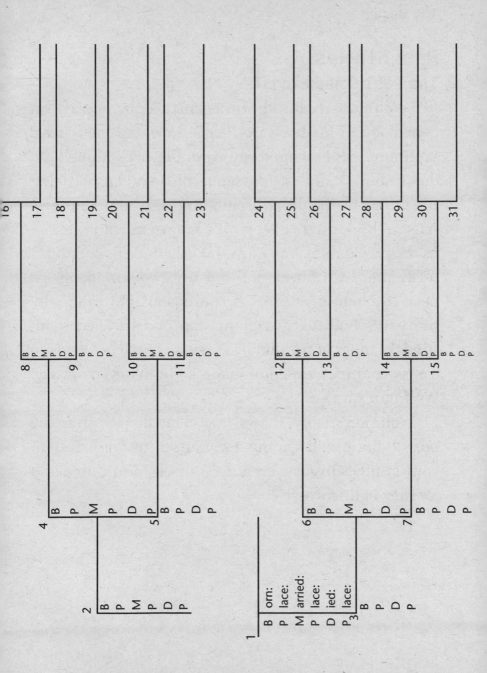

## Real Stories:
### The Past Comes to Life

Ira Wolfman recalls the moment he got hooked on genealogy in his book *Do People Grow on Family Trees?* Wolfman was looking for his grandfather's name on a dusty ship's manifest (passenger list). When he found the name, he discovered something else as well: a new sense of his family's history. "I'd known my grandfather as a kind old man who moved slowly and spoke English softly and with an accent. But until this moment, I'd never thought of him as a courageous boy who—by himself!—had taken a giant ship and traveled thousands of miles in the middle of winter to move forever to a new country whose language he didn't even speak," Wolfman says.

Wolfman's story shows how genealogy brings the past to life. You'll see this for yourself as you research your family's history. Prepare yourself for an amazing journey of discovery!

## Section 2
## Uncovering
## Your Roots

**BY NOW,** you're probably getting mighty curious. You're realizing that your family has a story. You're wondering what you'll discover by poking around in the past.

We can't give you any specific answers, of course. **Your relatives and your history are unique.** We *can,* however, give you a few clues. In this section, you'll learn about the types of information most genealogists hope to find. **Where** did your family come from, way back when? **Why** and **how** did they migrate? **What** were they like? The answers to these and other questions paint a picture of your past. Prepare to create some genealogical art!

# Where in the World?

Most genealogists want to know **where** their families came from. The first European settlers stepped onto what is now American soil (in what is now Plymouth, Massachusetts) in the year 1620. Since then, more than sixty million immigrants of every imaginable nationality have joined them. **Your ancestors may have been part of this big crowd.** (Unless you are 100 percent pure Native American, that is. But few people can make this claim.)

What caused this mass migration? Well, America is a popular place. Its laws guarantee religious and political freedom for all citizens. Also, its economic system allows people to earn money and get ahead in life. Over the centuries, these qualities have drawn many people to America's shores.

## First to Arrive

America's first European settlers arrived in 1620 on a ship called the *Mayflower*. Of the 102 people who made this journey, twenty-nine still have living relatives today. An estimated thirty million Americans are direct descendants of these founding fathers and mothers!

## Why Did They Come?

So did your ninth great-grandfather just wake up one day and think, *Hmmm, America. I wonder if I should uproot my whole family and check it out?* Probably not. Moving across the world is a huge deal. Most people had good reasons to **emigrate** (leave their home countries). Discovering these reasons is a fascinating part of your genealogical research.

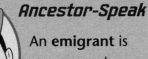
Here are the main reasons people move from one country to another. Which ones apply to *your* family?

- War and its aftermath
- Political or religious oppression
- Economic problems
- Natural disasters
- Famine and drought
- Following other family members
- Forced relocation (due to slavery, criminal activity, and so on)
- Adoption

## How Did They Get Here?

Until the mid-1900s, the majority of U.S. immigrants came from Europe. All of these immigrants had to cross the Atlantic Ocean—and they all did it by ship.

A fifteen-year-old Irish girl named Annie Moore was the first immigrant to pass through Ellis Island. She arrived in America on January 1, 1892.

Many immigration ships were crowded and dirty. Passengers were crammed into below-deck holds with dozens or even hundreds of other people. Sometimes there were no assigned spots, or even storage rooms for luggage. People huddled wherever they could, doing their best to keep their meager possessions safe.

Some of your ancestors may have arrived on ships like these. With a little research, you may be able to find the names and even photos of these ships. You might also discover whether your ancestors traveled alone, or with their entire families. Maybe you'll get *really* lucky and find

### A Record-breaking Year

Immigration to the United States peaked in 1907. Nearly 1.3 million new residents arrived during this record-breaking year.

diaries or letters that describe these experiences. These documents are like treasure troves for any genealogist.

## Ports of Entry

Immigration ships set sail from ports all over Europe. Many of them headed for New York City. From 1820 to 1892, a port called Castle Garden processed immigrants arriving in Manhattan. More than ten million people entered the United States through this facility.

Many people did not survive the overseas trip to America. The years 1846 and 1847 were particularly deadly. During this period, one out of every seven travelers got sick and died on the way.

When Castle Garden closed in 1892, a facility called Ellis Island took over the New York traffic. Ellis Island turned out to be the busiest arrival port in U.S. history. It processed more than twelve million immigrants between 1892 and 1954. Today, about forty percent of all living Americans have an Ellis Island ancestor.

New York may have been the most popular port of entry, but it was far from the only one. Boston, Baltimore, Philadelphia, Charleston, New Orleans, and many other port cities processed foreign arrivals, too.

On the U.S. west coast, San Francisco welcomed many Asian and Pacific Islander immigrants.

Where did *your* ancestors land? When you discover your relatives' ports of entry, you will uncover an important piece of your family's story.

## By Foot, Car, or Air

In 1965, new laws made it easier for citizens of Central and South America to emigrate to the United States. This change caused a major shift in immigration patterns.

If you have Latino ancestry, your ancestors may have arrived more recently than those of people of European descent. And they probably didn't come by ship. Chances are they drove, flew, or sometimes even walked into the United States. Today, Miami and Los Angeles are the main points of entry for South American, Central American, and Caribbean immigrants.

## Where'd They Go?

Your ancestors' ship stories may be fascinating, but they are just a starting point. After your distant relatives arrived, they settled somewhere. Where in the nation did *your* ancestors wind up?

The answer to this question, it turns out, has a lot to do with your ancestors' countries of origin. Most immigrants sought out others of the same nationality to live near. It's not hard to see why. They wanted to be around people who spoke their language and had the same basic history, outlook, and lifestyle. It's a comfort-level thing.

Here are a few settlement patterns that helped to define the United States. Do any of them apply to your family?

- Many Irish and Italian immigrants settled in the New York, Boston, and Chicago areas.

- Many Norwegian and Swedish immigrants settled in Minnesota, North Dakota, and South Dakota.

- Many English and French immigrants settled in the Northeast and the upper Midwest.

- Many German immigrants settled in the Midwest or along the upper U.S. East Coast.

**Moving Around**

Not all moves are around-the-world extravaganzas. Has your family ever moved across the street, across town, or to another state? If so, why? It's easy and fun to discover the stories behind your own family's "emigration" patterns!

## Involuntary Immigrants

Between the 1600s and 1860, hundreds of thousands of Africans were brought to the United States against their will to work as slaves. These involuntary immigrants settled mostly in the southern part of the United States. Many of their descendants continue to live in the South today.

- Many Polish immigrants settled in Illinois and Wisconsin.

- Many Canadian immigrants settled somewhere along the Canada/U.S. border.

- Many Central American immigrants settled somewhere along the Mexico/U.S. border.

- Many Chinese and Japanese immigrants settled in California.

- The majority of Cuban immigrants settled in south Florida.

**Did You Know?**

The U.S. Homestead Act of 1862 gave free land to anyone willing to farm it. This offer drew many immigrants to the United States.

## What's in a Name?

So you've thought a little bit about where your ancestors came from. Now you're wondering what else you can find out. Well, guess what? Everyone, **including you**, has a key piece of genealogical information at their fingertips. This information appears on your birth certificate, your medical records, and your report cards. It's even on your magazine subscriptions. **It's your surname.**

Chances are that you've never thought much about your surname. It's just something you were born with, like your fingers or that small mole on your back. But your surname is actually a gem of ancestral knowledge. Centuries ago, people earned surnames because of things they did, or places they lived, or how they looked, or a host of other reasons. So when you learn your surname's meaning, you'll learn something about your family's history as well.

About 90 percent of all American surnames fall into one of four categories. Which category includes *your* name?

*Job titles.* Many surnames describe an ancestor's occupation. Smith, Hunter, and Shoemaker are examples of occupational surnames. So are foreign-language versions of these and other job-related words. In German, for instance, "Smith" is "Schmidt." In Arabic, it's "Haddad."

*Places.* Some people's surnames refer to places. Hillman and English are examples of place-related surnames.

*Nicknames.* Sometimes people's surnames refer to habits, looks, or other personal traits. You already know that the names Bieber and Swift fall into this category. So does Jolie, which means "pretty" in French.

*Parentage.* Many surnames indicate an ancestor's parentage. "Peterson," for example, means "son of Peter." Ways of indicating parentage differ from country to country. In Ireland, for instance, it's "O'" (O'Brien = son of Brien). In England, a simple "s" does the job (Roberts = son of Robert).

**Did You Know?**

The surname "Gomez" is popular in Mexico. So it is no surprise to discover that actress Selena Gomez has Mexican roots.

## Changing Names

Your surname may be a key to your family's past. It isn't set in stone, though. Because guess what? Somewhere along the line, **your surname may have changed**. That's right. You may be a "Smith" now, but your ancestors might have gone by "Smythe" or "Schmidt" or "Szymczyk." (And yes, just in case you think we're making that up, "Szymczyk" *is* an actual name!)

Surnames can change for many reasons. The most common ones include:

*Translation.* Arabic, Chinese, and many other languages use a different lettering system than English. When surnames from these languages are translated into English, they can be spelled various ways. A Chinese surname whose English meaning is "gold," for instance, may be spelled "Jin," "Chin," "Kim," or "Kam."

*Mistakes.* Oops! An immigration official spelled your

**Ancestor-Speak**

A woman's surname prior to marriage is called her **maiden name**.

**Go for Four**

Your own surname is not the only one that matters. There are tons of surnames in your family tree, and they **all** apply to you. You can quadruple your fun by studying all four of your grandparents' surnames—and that's just for starters!

great-great-grandfather's name wrong, and the error stuck.

**Americanization.** Sometimes immigrants wanted their names to sound more American. So the German name "Bieber," for instance, could have become "Beaver." Hmmm, Justin Beaver. Catchy!

### Oops!

On this loan application from 1899, the applicant's last name is spelled two different ways. Simple mistakes like this one can be passed down through many generations.

Has *your* surname changed? If so, why? The story behind your current name might just be a fascinating part of your family's tale!

## Surnames: The Greatest Hits

According to the 2000 U.S. Census, the ten most common surnames in the United States are:

- Smith (~2.38 million)
- Johnson (~1.86 million)
- Williams (~1.53 million)
- Brown (~1.38 million)
- Jones (~1.36 million)
- Miller (~1.13 million)
- Davis (~1.07 million)
- Garcia (~858,000)
- Rodriguez (~804,000)
- Wilson (~783,000)

Top surnames in other countries include Murphy (Ireland), Hansen (Norway), Smirnov (Russia), Garcia (Spain), Rossi (Italy), González (Argentina and Chile), Sato (Japan), Cohen (Israel), and Nguyen (Vietnam).

In terms of volume, however, none of these names comes anywhere close to the world's top moniker. The most common surname anywhere is Wang. As of 2007, nearly ninety-three million Chinese nationals bore this name.

## Working for a Living

Surnames are tantalizing hints about the past. But that's *all* they are: **hints**. For true insight about your family's history, you need **facts**, such as your ancestors' **professions**.

Genealogists love profession information because it's fairly easy to find and it is revealing. **Think about it.** Let's say your great-great-uncle was a coal miner. You never met the man. Still, you can assume that he worked long hours in tough conditions, and that he never got rich. You might guess that he always had coal dust under his fingernails, and that he suffered from certain coal miner–specific illnesses. You can also be pretty sure that he didn't have a tan. You know all these things just from your ancestor's job title. Neat, eh?

In some families, anything goes when it comes to job histories. You might uncover many different professions. In other families, you'll find the same type of work popping up over and over again. Some professions are more likely than others to create family "dynasties." Do any of the following examples apply to *your* family?

## Entertaining Personalities

The entertainment field is jam-packed with famous families. The Barrymore clan, for instance, has been churning out actors for four generations. Actress Drew Barrymore is still making popular films today.

The Coppola family has a similar history. This dynasty includes director Francis Ford Coppola, director Sofia Coppola, actors Nicolas Cage and Jason Schwartzman, and many other famous folk.

Some of today's hottest young actors and musicians are following in a single family member's footsteps. Singer Miley Cyrus, for instance, is the daughter of Billy Ray Cyrus. Billy Ray had a successful country music career long before Miley came along. Actress Demi Lovato's mom was a country music singer, too. And actress Jamie Lynn Spears is singer Britney Spears's little sister.

## Serving Their Country

Many families have proud traditions of military service. In the royal family of the United Kingdom, for instance, nearly all young men enlist for at least a short time. Prince Charles did stints in both the Royal Air

## From Generation to Generation

These professions often run in families. Do any of them apply to you?

- Agriculture
- Medicine
- Religion
- Firefighting
- Police work
- Teaching
- Sports
- Seafaring

Force and Royal Navy. His sons, Princes William and Harry, have served as well. Charles's brother, Prince Andrew, spent more than twenty years in the Royal Navy.

In the United States, the Patton name is well represented in military circles. Three generations of Pattons, including the famous general George S. Patton, Jr., are famous for their military service.

U.S. Senator John McCain is also part of a military clan. McCain's father and grandfather were both admirals in the U.S. Navy. McCain himself fought in the Vietnam War. He turned to politics after a rough naval career that included nearly six years as a prisoner of war in North Vietnam.

## Born Leaders

While we're on the subject of politics, let's talk about political dynasties for a moment. The call to serve is strong in some families. It is quite common for a politician's siblings, parents, or other relatives to be big players in the political scene.

In America, the Kennedy family is about as big as it gets. More than twenty members of this clan have served in Washington, D.C., or other political circles. High-ranking family members include former U.S. President John F. Kennedy, former U.S. Senator Ted Kennedy, and former California Governor Arnold Schwarzenegger, who married into the Kennedy clan in 1986.

The Bush family is another important name in American politics. George H. W. Bush served as U.S. President from 1989–93.

### The Family Business

Family businesses are companies started by one family member, who then hires other family members to help. These businesses are sometimes passed down through generations. Is there a family business in your clan? What is it called and what does it do? How long has it been operating? Which family members have worked there? The answers to these questions are an important part of your family's history.

### It Runs in the Family

Taylor Swift's maternal grandmother, Margaret Finlay, is a professional opera singer. Taylor may have inherited some of her talent from this family source.

His oldest son, George W. Bush, held the same position from 2001–09. Another son, Jeb Bush, was Governor of Florida from 1999–2007.

## It Runs in the Family

Your relatives may not be famous entertainers, soldiers, or politicians. But then again, they might! You never know what you'll find when you go climbing in your family tree. That's part of what makes genealogy so much fun.

So what's the story with *your* family? Find out what your ancestors did for a living. Then read up on those professions. You'll have a whole new appreciation for your family heritage . . . **guaranteed**.

## Heroes and Villains

When you peer into the past, you'll probably learn more than just your ancestors' job descriptions. You'll also get glimpses of their lives and personalities. You may even discover that your family tree contains a few heroes. Yes, **heroes**!

What defines a family hero? In genealogy, it's basically any ancestor who makes you feel proud. People can become family heroes for many reasons. Do any of these examples apply to *your* family?

*Fame.* It's super cool to have a famous relative! Even if you don't know, say, Robert Pattinson from *Twilight* personally, you might love to discover if you are his eleventh cousin twice removed.

### A Real Saint

One of actress Brooke Shields's ancestors was a saint—yes, a real one! Shields is descended from King Louis IX of France, who was sainted soon after his death in 1270.

*Extraordinary feats.* Maybe your military grandfather earned a medal for wartime bravery. Or perhaps your third cousin set a world record for long-distance yodeling. Family members like these *definitely* give you bragging rights.

*Everyday heroism.* Maybe your great-great-great-aunt was a tireless charity worker or an advocate for women's rights. It's always great to discover everyday heroes in your family tree.

## The Flip Side

Families don't just contain heroes, of course. They may also include ancestors you're not totally thrilled to claim. Here are a few uncomfortable truths genealogists sometimes uncover.

*Crime and jail time.* Crime is nothing new. People have been breaking the law—and getting punished for it—for centuries.

*Rejection.* People have been expelled from school, excommunicated from church, and court-martialed from the military.

*General bad behavior.* Every family has 'em—the members who can't hold down a job, or who get married seven times, or who just generally raise eyebrows through their actions or lifestyles. Eek!

### Escaping the Past

According to a recent news report, evil German dictator Adolf Hitler has thirty-nine living descendants. All thirty-nine have changed their last names from Hitler to variants such as Hiedler or Hüttler.

Are there any "villains" in your family tree? **Get ready to find out!** This can be a touchy subject in some families, so tread gently. But just remember, it's all in the past. So keep your mind open to any possibility. When you do, you can build a more complete picture of your family's history.

## The "Boring" Ones

Heroes and villains are fascinating. Most of your ancestors, though, may not fall into these categories. They'll just be regular people with regular lives. Pretty boring, right?

**Wrong!** Everyday folk can be just as interesting as outrageous ones. Okay, so maybe your ancestors didn't have glamorous Hollywood connections or *CSI*–worthy lives of crime. But they had families, jobs, and stories. They were part of their communities, just like you're a part of *your* community today. Take the time to learn about your "boring" ancestors. You'll quickly see how ho-hum facts bring your family history to life.

There are endless examples of this idea. Here are just a few to get you started.

*Family size.* Some of your ancestors might have had a dozen brothers and sisters. Others might have been only children. Think about what it would be like to live in each ancestor's circumstances. Think about it from their parents' and children's perspectives, too.

*Religious affiliation.* Were your ancestors active in any religious community? If so, you can make a lot of good guesses about their lifestyles and beliefs.

### Ancestor-Speak

A **family history** is any genealogical investigation that involves stories as well as facts.

*Historic tidbits.* By this, we mean any nugget of information that ties your ancestors to historic events or situations. You can learn a lot from these nuggets. Did someone fight in a specific battle? Learn about that battle so you can "see" it through your ancestor's eyes. Do you have Japanese heritage? Learn about the struggles Japanese-Americans faced during World War II. These topics and countless others will help you to understand your family's journey through history . . . and they'll shed some light on *your* place in the big picture, too.

| | | 6.—Stock and Implements Owned by Borrower. | | |
|---|---|---|---|---|
| Horses _10_ | Mules _1_ | Cows _10_ | Other cattle _77_ | |
| Hogs _5_ | Sheep | Value of Stock? $ _1500_ | | What farming |
| _Complete outfit_ | | | | |
| Are there any chattel mortgages on any of this property? _no_ | | | Amounts of such mort | |
| By whom held? _no_ | | | | |

This document lists the livestock on a long-ago Kansas farm. What do you think it might have been like to tend this group of animals?

# Real Stories:
## Whitewashing the Past

In a 2009 letter, one genealogist explained some gaps in his family tree. "What I have deciphered so far is accurate, but may not be complete," he said. "I remember my [grandmother] telling me that a great-aunt of mine had traced our family tree, but sanitized it. Granny always claimed that this aunt deleted reference to some horse thieves and other undesirables. . . . I just wish I had been interested when [my aunts] were alive. I'm sure they knew a lot of our history, which is now lost." Luckily, not *everything* was lost. This genealogist managed to trace one family line back to the early seventeenth century.

## Section 3
## All in the Family

**IN THE PREVIOUS SECTION,** you discovered a few of the things genealogy might teach you. Are you intrigued? **You should be!** Your family history is just sitting there, waiting to be discovered. It's like a not-too-hidden treasure that anyone (read: YOU) can unearth.

So let's get digging! In this section, you'll learn how and where to begin your genealogical treasure hunt. You'll assemble your personal records. You'll also talk to relatives, leaf through family photo albums, and maybe check out a few musty documents. All of these activities are easy and fun—as you're about to find out for yourself. Get ready to take the first steps on your personal genealogical journey!

## Start with Yourself

At this point, your ancestors are mysteries. By comparison, **you** are an open book. You know your name, your birth date, your address, and all that other good stuff. It might seem pointless to investigate yourself.

**But it isn't.** Far from it! As many genealogists have discovered, knowing yourself is an essential part of the journey. It's also an *easy* part, since you have access to pretty much any personal records you could ever need.

So, start with yourself. With a parent's help, gather your birth records, identification documents, and other key information. (See the list on the next page for ideas.) You'll get some practice that will come in handy when the time comes to dig a little deeper. And who knows? You

### Ancestor-Speak

The key facts about a person's life—including birth, marriage, and death dates—are called **vital statistics**.

| | DEPARTMEN |
|---|---|
| | VITAL ST |
| | CERTIFICATI |
| DATE OF BIRTH  1-2-67 (MO. DAY, YEAR, HOUR) | 12:07 p.m. |
| CITY, BOROUGH, OR TOWNSHIP OF BIRTH  PITTSBURGH | |
| COUNTY OF BIRTH  ALLEGHENY | |

One genealogist was excited to find her exact time of birth on her birth certificate.

might even uncover some interesting or surprising facts. You wouldn't be the first genealogist to discover that you don't know yourself quite as well as you think!

## Gather This Information

Here's a starter list of the personal information you should gather. Feel free to add anything you think might be important or interesting to future generations.

- Full name

- Nicknames (if any)

- Date and time of birth

- Place of birth

- Birth announcement, if your parents sent one out

- Copy of birth certificate

- Copy of Social Security card

- Copy of passport's ID page (if you have a passport)

- Copy of newborn footprints/handprints/fingerprints

- Current address

- Past addresses

- Names of your schools

- Full names of all siblings and parents

- Your religious affiliation (if any)

- School report cards

- Printed stories relating to you (i.e., newspaper birth announcements, etc.)

## Family Records

So you've dug up your own vital information. Great job! Now it's time to move on to the second-easiest step. You're going to look for information that concerns your parents, grandparents, siblings, and other immediate

### Where to Look

Where do people stash their old stuff? Here are some classic hidey-holes. With permission, do a little document digging in these places. You might just find some long-forgotten treasures.

- In the attic

- In the basement

- In the garage

- Under the bed or other furniture

- In closets

- In junk drawers

- In filing cabinets

- On bookshelves

- In safes

- On top of bureaus and other tall pieces of furniture

relatives. And the best part is, you're going to do it **under your own roof.**

Sounds almost too easy, doesn't it? But make no mistake. Many homes are treasure troves of genealogical information. Your parents may have been saving documents, tax records, photos, and other interesting stuff for years. If you're really lucky, they might have saved boxes full of your grandparents' or great-grandparents' stuff, too.

With a parent's permission and help, go through old files and other storage spots in your home. Look for things that provide clues to your family's past. Chances are good that you'll discover more than you ever imagined.

## Info Etiquette

Never, ever go poking through someone's personal stuff without permission. **Ever.**

## On the Hunt

So what exactly are you looking for? The next few pages will give you some ideas. Don't be limited by these suggestions, though. Anything that provides information is a valuable find.

*Vital documents.* Birth, death, and marriage certificates provide a wealth of information. Because these documents are official and difficult to replace, people tend to hold on to them for generations. Don't be surprised if you find some really old stuff in this particular pile.

*The family Bible.* An old family Bible can be a good source of vital statistics, too. In earlier generations, many families jotted key events inside the front or back covers of these books.

*Identification items.* Old driver's licenses, passports, college ID cards, Social Security cards, and similar items can help you to pin down many key pieces of information. Passports are especially interesting because they tell you about an ancestor's travels.

*Financial documents.* Loan applications, bills, tax returns, and other official documents provide both hard facts (like names and addresses) and lifestyle clues (like income levels and spending habits).

*Letters and postcards.* Personal communications are invaluable information sources, if you're willing to do a little reading.

***Photo collections.*** That old photo album or box of loose photos that's been collecting dust on the top shelf for two decades? Open it up! It's fun to see pictures of your ancestors. Don't forget to check the backs of the photos for written names, dates, and places.

***Baby books.*** What was your grandfather's first word? Did your great-grandmother have a favorite stuffed toy, and if so, what was its name? When did your dad lose his first tooth? These fun facts and countless others can be found in baby books.

***Memorabilia.*** The term "memorabilia" means items saved for sentimental reasons. Examples include ticket stubs, brochures, old report

## Old = Good

When it comes to clue hunting, older is usually better. That threadbare plush duck you found? It didn't get that way from sitting on a shelf. One of your ancestors **adored** it as a child. Treasure the grimy pieces of memorabilia you find during your search. They're priceless pieces of the past!

## Other People's Homes

Once you've turned your own home upside down, continue your quest at relatives' homes. (We'll say it again: **Get Permission First.**) Remember, your parents aren't the only ones with information stashes!

**Did You Know?**

People in antique photos usually look like sourpusses. That's because they weren't allowed to smile! Old-fashioned cameras had long exposure times. People couldn't hold a smile in place long enough for the camera to capture a focused image.

cards, baby teeth, or other things that are valuable because of the memories they hold. Every piece of memorabilia has a story to tell. When you learn these stories, you may learn something about yourself as well.

*Old newspapers and magazines.* People save newspapers and magazines only if they're important in some way. So go through each printed piece carefully. See if you can figure out why your ancestor saved this particular item.

## I Remember . . .

Old documents are useful sources of information. When it comes to getting the real scoop, though, nothing beats **actual, living people**. We're talking, of course, about your relatives—especially the older ones. A grandparent or even a great-grandparent, if you're lucky enough to have one living, knows family stories that no document could ever match.

It isn't hard to access these stories. Most people love to talk about themselves and their family histories. In fact, countless genealogists have discovered that it can be tough to make people **stop** talking once they start. So go

### The Five Ws

Ask questions beginning with the five Ws—Who? What? When? Where? Why?—to spark memories during an interview.

ahead—don't be nervous! **Ask** the questions, then sit back and **listen** to the answers. Your relatives will be happy to chat, and you may be fascinated with the information they share. It's a win-win situation for everyone. And that's *always* the best way to do things!

## Preparing for the Interview

Technically speaking, historic gab sessions are interviews. And every professional knows that interviews go better when you're prepared. So let's prepare! Here are a few good ways to get ready for your genealogical chats.

*Make an appointment.* Don't just call Granny out of the blue and start firing questions at her. Explain in advance what you're doing, when you want to do it, and how long you think it will take. Your interviewees will be more cooperative if you're not interrupting their

### Record It

Record your genealogical interviews on film or any audio medium if you possibly can. Recording is important because it lets you really **listen** during the interview without worrying about what you might forget. Review the recording later to nail down the details of your conversation.

weekly card game or favorite television show.

*Consider the source.* What is unique about your interviewee? What special information might this person contribute to your research? Remember, you can't ask everything. So it can be helpful to focus on one area of your family history.

*List your questions.* Brainstorm a list of questions you'd like to ask during your interview. Write them all down so you won't forget anything. This list will keep your interview on track.

## Conducting the Interview

When your prep work is done, it's time to conduct your interview. It's best to talk face-to-face. If your interviewee lives far away, though, you might have to do your interview over the phone. You could also use a video-conferencing service, such as Skype, if both you and your interviewee are comfortable with that.

Whatever method you choose, there are things you can do to make sure your interview goes smoothly. Here are some tried-and-true tips.

*Ask, ask, ask.* Interviewers are allowed and even expected to be pests (as long as you're nice about it, of course). If you're not getting the answers you need, ask the same questions in another way. You might have to try a few times before you uncover the facts you're seeking.

*Be friendly.* Yes, you have a job to do. But you should still be friendly and chatty. If you treat your interview like a fun conversation, your interviewee will tell you more.

### Ancestor-Speak

An **interviewer** is the person who conducts an interview.

An **interviewee** is the person being interviewed.

*Be flexible.* Your interview might veer away from your question list. That's okay. In genealogy, any information is good information. If you're getting the scoop, just go with the flow!

### Thanks a Lot!

It's always nice to send thank-you notes to your interviewees. Let them know how much you appreciate their help!

## After the Interview

You've conducted a successful interview and learned some fascinating things. Great job, genealogist! But don't stop just yet. You have a few loose ends to tie up before you can call your interview complete.

Your main job, of course, is to identify key facts and incorporate them into your research. To do this, go over your notes after the interview. Or, if you recorded it, watch or listen to the recording. Write down anything important. This is the easiest way to create a written record of the things your interviewee said.

Sometimes the review process raises new questions. You might realize, for instance, that you forgot to ask your uncle Al for a certain date or name. Jot these things down. Then call back your interviewee and ask for just a few more minutes of his or her time. As long as you ask politely, people should be happy to help you fill in the gaps.

# Written Requests

As you get deeper into your research, you may find that your immediate family can't answer all of your questions. You might decide, therefore, to ask some other relatives for help.

### Ancestor-Speak

A person who tells you about something he or she personally experienced is called a **primary source.**

"Other relatives" fall into two categories. Category One includes the relatives you know, kind of. (You met your second cousin Bonnie at a picnic once. Your great-aunt Matilda sends you a birthday card now and then.) Category Two includes relatives you know *about*, but have never actually met or had contact with in any way.

It can be awkward to phone people in either of these categories. For one thing, you might feel shy. But more importantly, it's not good to take people by surprise. You'll get more information if your distant relatives know **who you are** and **what you want** before you start

### Spring for the Stamps

Always include a self-addressed stamped envelope (SASE) when asking someone to write you back. It's the polite thing to do!

## Instant Family Tree

The online social network Facebook has revolutionized the genealogy field. Here's how it works. With a parent's permission, you become Facebook "friends" with the relatives you know. These people may be "friends" with other relatives you *don't* know. Facebook links all these relationships and tells everyone about each other. Before you know it, you're buddies with distant cousins you never knew existed!

asking them for personal information. So a little introduction is in order first.

## Snail Mail or E-Mail

Written communication is an answer to this problem. Traditionally, genealogists have used snail mail to contact their distant relatives. In recent years, e-mail has become more popular. Either method is fine. Just make sure you follow a few simple guidelines to get the most out of your written exchanges.

*Introduce yourself.* Explain exactly who you are and how you're related to the letter recipient. Also explain how you got the person's contact information.

*State your goals.* Explain that you are researching your family tree and that you are looking for certain types of information.

*Make your request.* Ask for permission to call, or to send more information. If you have just a few simple questions, you could include them in your letter and ask for them to be answered by return mail.

*Guarantee confidentiality.* Make it clear that you will keep your communication private. Remember, you're asking for personal information that people might hesitate to give out.

**Who and When**

Most genealogists keep a contact sheet. They write down **who** they wrote to and **when** they did it. They may also describe, briefly, **what** they wrote. When a reply comes in, the genealogist marks that on the contact sheet, too. It's a simple but effective way to keep track of your correspondence.

*Express your thanks.* End your letter with a sincere thank-you. It never hurts to be nice when you're asking for favors!

## A Sample Letter

Janelle Simmons
123 Maple Lane
Anytown, USA
Phone: 555-1234
E-mail: Janelle@anycom.com

Dear Mr. Meier,

   You don't know me, but we're related! My grandfather, George Simmons, is your second cousin. That makes me your second cousin twice removed. My father, Gregory Simmons, gave me your address. He thought you might be willing to tell me a few things about our family's history. I sure hope he's right! ☺

   I've included a separate sheet of paper with a few questions. Would you mind answering the questions and returning the sheet to me? You could call or e-mail me, if you prefer. My parents know you might be contacting me. Anything you tell me is confidential, of course.

   I am excited to get your answers. Our family is fascinating, don't you think? Thank you so much for your help!

                                   Sincerely,
                                   Janelle Simmons

## A Word of Caution

They say elephants never forget. **Lucky elephants.** Their genealogical research would be a lot easier than yours (if elephants could do research, that is).

Because here's the thing. People *do* forget, and they do it all the time. Even worse, they often replace the missing memories with false information. Usually they don't even realize their mistakes. They "know" those wrong facts, and they'll repeat them to anyone who will listen. And they'll be absolutely, positively, 100 percent convinced that they are right.

### Both Sides of the Story

Different people remember things differently. Want proof? Ask two relatives to tell you the same family story. You'll be amazed at the variation. This little exercise proves how easy it is to get things wrong. **Don't let it happen to you.** Verify, verify, verify your facts!

**But don't let them convince YOU.** No, we're not saying you shouldn't trust your interviewees. We're just saying keep an open mind. Listen to everything your relatives say. Write it down. Believe it—**mostly**. Then double- and triple-check it with other sources, if you can. When *every* available source agrees, you can feel confident that your data is correct.

## What's the Big Deal?

So what's the big deal? Does it honestly matter if you misspell a name or get the occasional date wrong? After all, little errors like these don't really change anything. Your family stories will be the same no matter what year they happened, right?

**This is true.** And we can't deny it: Careless genealogists have just as much fun as thorough ones. But think about what you're doing for a moment. You—yes, **you personally**—are in charge of a few precious parts of your family's history. Future generations may depend on these chunks. It would be nice if they were accurate, don't you think?

Here's the bottom line: **Don't be careless.** You're a genealogist now, and true genealogists care about the details. Take the time to do things right. You can feel good about doing your best work—and future generations will thank you for it, too.

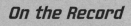

*On the Record*

Check spoken facts against official documents (birth certificates, passports, and so on) whenever possible. It's the only way to be sure!

# Get It Together

In this section, you've examined old documents, conducted interviews, and written to distant relatives. Congratulations, genealogist! Your pile of family facts is growing.

And growing . . . and growing . . . and growing. Wow, that sure is a lot of information you've got there. **Now what are you going to do with it?**

That's the big question for every genealogist. Sure, facts are fantastic and stories are super. But unless you organize those facts and stories in a way that makes sense, you'll **lose track** of them. You'll **forget** how they relate to each other. After all your hard work, you really don't want this to happen.

## Genealogy Software

These top-rated genealogy programs are inexpensive but invaluable. They can help you to organize your research.

- Legacy
- Family Tree Maker
- RootsMagic
- Ancestral Quest
- Family Historian

That's why organization is essential for genealogists. No, it isn't the most exciting part of the process—but

## Anything Goes

Any organization system is better than none. Use whatever method works for **you**.

it's one of the most important. Here are a few ways to keep yourself and your research on track.

***Get a system.*** Make some kind of system for sorting your work into logical chunks. Photos, documents, tape recordings, and other "hard" items can be stored in well-labeled file folders and boxes. Names, dates, and other data can be entered into computer programs. There are lots of helpful genealogy software packages available. Choose one that has the features you need.

***Cite your sources.*** You don't just need to organize your information. You need to remember where it came from, too. Always write down your sources. That way, you'll be able to recheck anything at any time.

***Do it now.*** Quickness is a key part of being organized. Right now, you remember where you found Grandpa Elliott's high-school diploma. Two months from now, you might not. So take care of it now. Sort it, label it, store it, do whatever you have to do. Just don't let your paperwork pile up!

# Real Stories:
## On the Record

In her book *Who Do You Think You Are?: The Essential Guide to Tracing Your Family History*, genealogist Megan Smolenyak tells the following story:

"I fortunately did tape-record a conversation with my nana when she was ninety years old. As we often do, I somehow expected her to live forever, but she passed away three months later. As we chatted, I urged her to tell me the family stories I had heard so many times growing up that they almost bored me—you know, the ones that make everyone groan? When I finally mustered the nerve to listen to the tape (it can take a while after losing a loved one), I was stunned by how much my mind had already managed to jumble. I thought I knew these stories by heart, but I already had some of the details wrong."

This incident shows how important it is to record personal interviews. It's a simple step that will keep your memories—and your research—from going astray.

## Section 4
## Digging Deeper

**YOU'VE OPENED MUSTY SHOEBOXES** and crawled through cobweb-filled attics. You've talked to every relative you know, and you've written to a few you don't. In short, you've exhausted your immediate family's knowledge and resources. But **you're hooked on genealogy.** You want **more, more, more.**

So now what?

Plenty, that's what! There are countless ways to find extra information about your ancestors. Thousands of books, libraries, museums, and computer archives hold the facts you crave. This section will talk about these resources—**what** they are, **where** they are, and **how** to get them. Are you ready to go above and beyond? Then turn the page. Let's dig a little deeper into your family's history!

# The Paper Trail

When your parents got married, someone wrote it down. When you were born, someone wrote it down. And if you ever applied for a passport, guess what? Yep, someone wrote that down, too.

For hundreds of years, things have been like that. Major life events create paperwork. Luckily for genealogists everywhere, this paperwork usually hangs around for a long, long time. It serves as a permanent and useful record of your ancestors' lives.

Anyone, **including you**, can tap into this record. You just need to know where to look. The next few pages list the most important genealogical resources. When you find any one of these documents, you'll find a piece of your family's past as well.

*Birth records.* Birth records include all kinds of great information. At the very least, they'll give you the baby's name and gender; the parents' names, including the mother's maiden name; and the baby's birth date and place. Some birth records also include information about the parents' races, occupations, or other interesting facts.

*Marriage certificates.* Marriage certificates give you

the full names and addresses of the bride and groom. They also list the wedding date and place and usually the name of the person who performed the ceremony. Marriage certificates are the *only* wedding-related documents you can trust completely. All other records—newspaper articles, marriage licenses, and so on—should be considered clues, not proof.

*Death certificates.* Death certificates tell you when and where a person died. They usually list the cause of death as well. They may include the deceased's most recent address, birthplace, or other personal information.

**Ancestor-Speak**

A person who has passed away is known as the **decedent** or the **deceased**.

*Cemetery records.* Once a person dies, he or she is buried or cremated. Cemeteries and crematories keep files on these events. If you know an ancestor's final resting place, contact the administrators and ask to see your ancestors' records. Chances are good that your request will be honored.

*Census records.* In the United States, a survey of all residents is done once every ten years. This survey is called the census. Census records include a wealth of information about names, addresses, ethnicities, professions, extended families, and much more. By law, census data must be kept private for seventy-two years after it is collected. So this resource won't help if you're looking for recent information.

**Did You Know?**

Ships' passenger lists are jam-packed with spelling errors. Immigration officials did their best to write each person's name correctly, but they made a **lot** of mistakes.

*Passenger lists.* Also known as ships' manifests, these documents list every person who arrived on a certain vessel on a certain date. Before 1820, most passenger lists included names only. After 1820, lists were expanded to include age, gender, profession, and country of origin information for each passenger.

*Citizenship records.* After your ancestors came to the United States, they probably applied for citizenship. These applications are still on file, and they're full of information. They can be

**Ancestor-Speak**

The process of changing one's nationality is called **naturalization**. Documents that concern this process are called **naturalization papers.**

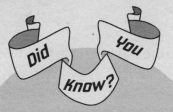

In America, all men must register for Selective Service when they reach age eighteen. However, no one has actually been drafted since 1973.

hard to find, though. They're mostly buried in local court-houses. So you'll need to identify the exact court system your ancestor used during his or her citizen-ship process.

***Military records.*** If your ancestor was in the military, there's a record of his or her service. Military records can include **all kinds** of interesting stuff. Even if your ancestor didn't serve, **he** may have registered for the U.S. Selective Service System, also called "the draft," at some point. (That's right, **he**. Women have never been drafted through the S.S.S.) Draft records can be a good source of basic information.

**The Missing Decade**

In 1921, a huge fire destroyed nearly all records from the 1890 U.S. Census. The resulting information gap is a constant problem for genealogists.

***The paper trail.*** We've hit the biggies. But really, we've just scratched the surface. People's everyday activities generate all kinds of documents. Diplomas, mortgages, wills, bank statements, and even phone books can be data gold mines. **It's all fair game.** Remember, any source is good if it fills a gap in your family tree!

## You Count!

The most recent U.S. Census was completed on April 1, 2010, and you may be on it! Chances are, your parent(s) provided your name, age, birthday, ethnicity, and even your home phone number. Don't worry about your privacy, though—at least, not yet. The 2010 Census won't become available to the public until April 1, 2082.

# Find It Online

So now you know **what** you're looking for. But you're still new to this genealogy thing, so you probably have no idea **where** to find it. How in the world are you going to get your hands on that certain marriage certificate, or military record, or ship's passenger list?

A mere decade ago, these could be tough tasks. Things are much easier now, though, thanks to the Internet. **There are countless genealogical databases online.** No, you can't find everything you need via your home computer. But you can find a **lot**—especially the basic stuff. So sign on to the Web. It's time to start your search!

## Where to Start

There's no way we can cover every genealogical site. There are far too many. But we *can* get you started. The sites on the next few pages are favorites of genealogists everywhere. They're sure to become your favorites, too!

**Ancestry.com** (www.ancestry.com)

Ancestry.com claims to be "the world's largest online resource for family history documents and family trees." By mid-2010, the site included more than four billion records! Its searchable collections include census lists, immigration records, news articles, vital statistics (birth, marriage, and death records), military records, and much more.

It's free to run basic searches or build a simple family tree on Ancestry.com. To use *all* of the site's features, you'll need to pay a yearly membership fee. Or you might get

### Filling the Gaps

There is a huge amount of genealogical information online—but it's only the tip of the iceberg. Most records are still on paper somewhere. Volunteers around the world are working to enter this information into computer databases. They hope that someday soon, genealogists will be able to look up practically anything from their home computers.

free access to the site through your local library. Check to see if your library offers this service.

## FamilySearch (www.familysearch.org)

This site is run by a faith organization called the Church of Jesus Christ of Latter-Day Saints (LDS). Ancestors are important in the LDS belief system. To help its members find these people, the Church has created the world's biggest genealogical library. FamilySearch is the online version of this collection.

FamilySearch doesn't include all of the LDS library's records. Not even close! But it has enough information to be useful, and it's free. So check it out. Maybe you'll get lucky and find the data you need.

## Heritage Quest Online
(www.heritagequestonline.com)

Heritage Quest is a good starting point for information about people, places, and publications. It is available through many libraries and other institutions. Check to see if your library subscribes to this service.

## Ellis Island
(www.ellisisland.org) and
## Castle Garden
(www.castlegarden.org)

Millions of people landed at Ellis Island and Castle Garden between 1830 and 1954. Some of these people were immigrants. Others were just passing through. Records for travelers of both types can be found online. The Ellis Island site is especially complete, and it's free. Check to see if your ancestors entered through this historic port.

## GenealogyBank
(www.genealogybank.com)

This site charges a membership fee. But if you're looking for old newspaper articles, it might be worth it. GenealogyBank's online collection goes all the way back to 1690 and covers all fifty U.S. states. You may find a fascinating story or two in this massive database.

## Digging Deeper

**Cyndi's List** (www.cyndislist.com)
Cyndi's List doesn't have any actual genealogical records. It just tells you where to find them. It does this by sorting more than 270,000 links into logical categories. Polar explorers? There's a category for that. Information about orphans? There's a category for that, too. In short, if you're looking for just about anything, this site will point you in the right direction. It's fun and it's free, so check it out.

### Ellis Island Arrivals

Ellis Island's website includes a list of famous immigrants and some travelers who were already American citizens. The list includes:

- Rudyard Kipling, author, 1892
- Charlie Chaplin, actor, 1912
- Charles Atlas, bodybuilder, 1903
- Harry Houdini, magician, 1914
- John Ringling, circus owner, 1906
- Walt Disney, entertainer, 1919
- Sigmund Freud, physician, 1909
- Albert Einstein, scientist, 1921

**Google** (www.google.com) and
**Yahoo!** (www.yahoo.com)

These are not genealogy sites. They're search engines that can help you find all kinds of information. Enter your ancestors' names and see what pops up. You might be pleasantly surprised!

## The Real Thing

Computer searches are a good start. Sooner or later, though, most genealogists run into research dead ends. **This may happen to you.** When it does, there's just one thing to do. You need to visit an actual library to find the information you want.

Luckily, tons of great genealogical archives are available to the public. Some of these archives might be in your own hometown. Others are in cities you might visit with your family someday. Either way, check out the following collections if you get the chance. You'll be glad you did!

**The Family History Library** (Salt Lake City, Utah)
When it comes to family history, this library is the main event! It's the biggest genealogical archive in the world, with more than 2.4 million rolls of microfilmed records, plus books, periodicals, newspapers, and many other

## Best Public Libraries

According to *Family Tree* magazine, the top ten public libraries for genealogy research are:

- Allen County Public Library (Fort Wayne, Indiana)

- Clayton Library Center for Genealogical Research (Houston, Texas)

- Birmingham Public Library (Birmingham, Alabama)

- Dallas Public Library (Dallas, Texas)

- Denver Public Library (Denver, Colorado)

- Detroit Public Library (Detroit, Michigan)

- Los Angeles Public Library (Los Angeles, California)

- Mid-Continent Public Library (Independence, Missouri)

- The New York Public Library (New York City, New York)

- Public Library of Cincinnati and Hamilton County (Cincinnati, Ohio) resources. This vast collection includes the residents of more than 110 nations.

Along with its Salt Lake City headquarters, the Family History Library has more than 4,500 branches. These branches are called "family history centers," and there's probably one near you. Family history centers don't have as many records as the main branch. But they do have a master catalog, and they can order documents for you. Visit any one of these centers for free genealogical help.

**Library of Congress** (Washington, D.C.)
The massive Library of Congress fills three whole buildings. It has more shelf space than any other library in the world, and it holds more than 140 million items. Many of these items are useful to genealogists. Will they be useful to *you*? Take a look and find out for yourself!

**The National Archives Building** (Washington, D.C.)
The U.S. National Archives and Records Administration (NARA) is in charge of preserving important American documents. The National Archives Building contains many of these documents, including census data, ships'

**Did You Know?**

The Library of Congress is open to the public, but only government officials are allowed to check out books.

passenger lists, U.S. military records, land records, and much more.

You must be at least fourteen years old to do research in the National Archives Building. Bring a grown-up if you haven't reached this age.

**New England Historic Genealogical Society** (Boston, Massachusetts)

The library of the New England Historic Genealogical Society holds more than twenty-eight million items. This collection focuses on New England–area ancestors, but it includes limited information about people in other regions as well. Many of the Society's records are online at www.newenglandancestors.org.

**American Family Immigration History Center** (AFIHC) (Ellis Island, New York)

All of Ellis Island's records are available online. So you don't really **need** to visit the facility's library to get the information you need. But you might **want** to, just for fun—especially if you have Ellis Island ancestors.

The AFIHC is part of the Statue of Liberty National Monument and can be reached only by ferry boat. It's a great way to tie facts and feelings into one fun visit!

## Your Local Library

Last but not least! Compared to the collections we've already discussed, your local library might not seem too impressive. But it's the easiest place to start. And if your family has lived in the same area for a long time, it may also be one of the best. Local newspapers and magazines might have mentioned your ancestors for one reason or another. These notices and stories provide information that you may not find anywhere else . . . and *that's* what genealogical research is all about.

### Learn More

Your local library probably has great genealogy how-to books. Borrow these books to get step-by-step instructions for researching your family history.

# Tricky Ancestries

Some lucky genealogists have an easy time tracing their family trees. Their ancestors arrived in the most common ways, and their movements are well documented. One trip to the library and all the pieces fall into place.

For most genealogists, however, the process is more difficult. Maybe a certain family's records are hard to find. Or maybe they don't even exist! Problems like these can be roadblocks to the research process.

Certain groups of people run into these roadblocks more often than others. Does your family fall into any of the categories on the next few pages? If so, you face a few challenges. But don't despair. Other genealogists have overcome these issues, and you also may be able to!

## Native American Heritage

Millions of people lived in North America before the first European settlers arrived. Many modern Americans are related to these people. It can be hard, however, to dig up Native American roots, since these peoples did not keep written records. In the 1800s, U.S. agents started keeping track of some, but not all, Native American tribes. You'll be lucky to get this far back in your research.

## Written in Your Genes

Every person has material called DNA inside his or her body. If two people provide samples of this material, scientists can compare the samples. They look for certain key similarities. If the similarities exist, the DNA's owners are probably related.

DNA testing has become more affordable in recent years. As a result, an increasing number of genealogists are using this service to fill gaps in their family tree. DNA can't tell you exactly *how* you're related to someone, but it can show whether or not *some* family connection exists. And sometimes that's enough—especially when written records don't do the job.

If you want to study your Native American roots, find your tribe's name and location first. Then contact the U.S. Bureau of Indian Affairs (www.bia.gov). This organization may be able to point you in the right direction.

## African Heritage

In the eighteenth and nineteenth centuries, more than 400,000 Africans came to America as slaves. If your ancestor was in this group,

### Ancestor-Speak

The word **lineage** refers to your line of descent from a specific ancestor.

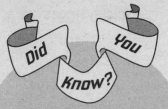

**Did You Know?**

The Jonas Brothers claim to have Cherokee blood. Their heritage is also Italian, German, and Irish.

a major research task lies ahead! African-Americans were not named in the U.S. Census until 1870 (although the names of all *free* African Americans were included in the 1850 and 1860 census). Some older records do exist, but they're hit or miss. You'll need luck and persistence to find them.

AfriGeneas (www.afrigeneas.com) is one good place to start your search. This organization maintains many online databases. It also hosts discussion forums and other useful tools. It has helped many people with African-American ancestry to find their roots. It may be able to help you, too.

## Jewish Heritage

At some point in their research, many people with European Jewish roots will discover relatives who died in the Holocaust (1939–45). More than six million Jews lost their lives during this event. These people also lost their property and their personal records. This destruction caused a huge gap in the world's genealogical record.

Many people are working to fill this gap. An

organization called JewishGen (www.jewishgen.org) is helping to coordinate the rebuilding effort. JewishGen had more than fourteen million records by mid-2010, and that number grows every day. So the chances of finding your European Jewish ancestors are getting better and better as time goes on.

## Early Arrivals

Some genealogists are proud of their Mayflower ancestors or other "early arrivals." Maybe that's because these people are so hard to find! The National Archives' arrivals collection only goes back to 1820. If your ancestors immigrated before that year, you'll have to search hard for their ship records.

### Remembering the Dead

After the Holocaust of World War II, groups of survivors, relatives, and friends got together to share their memories. They recorded these memories in volumes called Yizkor books. Most Yizkor books contain information about a certain town along with the people who lived there. They are usually written in Yiddish or Hebrew. If you know these languages, or know someone who does, Yizkor books could be a good resource for you.

It will be a big help if you know an ancestor's port of entry or ship's name. If you have this information, check with port or state officials. They may be able to provide the records you need.

## Adoption Issues

During your research, you may discover an adopted relative. Or you may be adopted yourself. Adoption poses special challenges for genealogists. Unless you know the names of the adopted person's birth parents, you won't get far with their "blood" family tree.

You can ask your parents or other adults for this information. But remember, adoption can be a sensitive issue in some families. So think carefully before tackling this task. If you *do* decide to move forward, tread gently. A little tact goes a long way!

### Help for Beginners

If you join only one organization, Ancestry.com is a good place to start. It has lots of useful tools and information, especially for beginners. Ask a grown-up for permission to join and for any setup help you need.

## Join the Club

By this point, you're probably getting the feeling that genealogy research can be a big job. **That's true. It can.** But the good news is, you don't have to do all of the work yourself. Other genealogists have already found many of the facts you need. They may be willing to share their research, if you'll share yours in return.

Exchanges like this usually happen through genealogy clubs. The members of these clubs are interested in a certain area of history, a certain family, or a certain ethnic heritage. They post their findings, answer each other's questions, and generally work toward a common goal. By doing these things, they make a big job a little bit easier for everyone involved.

## Types of Clubs

Genealogy clubs fall into three main categories:

*Surname clubs.* There are thousands of surname clubs. These organizations focus on one specific surname. Membership is usually open to anyone researching this name.

*Shared experiences.* Many genealogy clubs focus on ancestors who shared certain experiences. For example, there's a club for the descendants of California gold rush participants. Countless other clubs focus on other events.

*Ethnic heritage.* No matter what your ethnic heritage is, there's a genealogical club for you. These clubs are

### Prove It

Some hereditary societies are open to anyone who is interested. Others require members to have certain lineages. A prestigious group called Daughters of the American Revolution (DAR), for example, is open only to women whose ancestors helped the cause of American independence in the 1700s. Applicants must prove they have a qualified ancestor before they can be accepted into the DAR.

especially useful for people with deep roots in one specific culture.

It's easy to find a club that suits your needs. Just do a quick online search in your area of interest. Before you know it, you'll have as much help as you can handle. You might just make some new friends, too!

## Real Stories:
### A Great Pair of Genes

A famous singer named Jimmy Buffett and a famous financial advisor named Warren Buffett wondered for decades if they were related. They thought they must be, since they shared an uncommon last name. But years of genealogical research failed to turn up a link.

In 2007, the two men decided to end the mystery. They both sent DNA samples to a lab for analysis. The analysis showed that Jimmy's and Warren's genes were different. Scientists concluded that the men probably were not related.

Despite this result, the two Buffetts still treat each other like family. They call one another "Cousin Jimmy" and "Uncle Warren," and they attend social events together. Warren Buffett even performed music at a restaurant opening with his rock-star "relative" once. The men's relationship proves that family isn't just in your genes. It's in your heart as well.

## Section 5
## Now What?

**AT THIS POINT,** you have turned into quite the genealogist. You've collected stories and documents and articles and names and dates . . . whew! You're getting a pretty good handle on your family's history. And you may be excited about the things you have learned.

Well, prepare to get more excited! You can do some really fun things with the information you've gathered, and this section will show you how. Discover how to **share** your findings, **meet** long-lost relatives, **visit** the places where history happened, and much more. In one way, it's the final stage in your genealogical journey. But in another way, it's just the beginning. You're tying together the past and the present and writing a new chapter of your family's story. So what are you waiting for? Turn the page and let's get going!

# Share the News

It's fun to uncover your family's story. The *real* fun, however, starts when the research ends. Now's the **big moment** when you get to share your discoveries with your family, your friends, and anyone else who's interested.

The sharing phase of the genealogical process can be very satisfying. For one thing, researchers love to show off their hard work. **Well, of course. Who doesn't?** But there's more to it than just that. Genealogists appreciate the past, and they care deeply about preserving it. By spreading the word, they're doing their part to keep history alive.

There are countless ways to share genealogical findings. The next few pages explain some favorites. Choose the ones that work best for you and your family.

## Family Trees

Creating an artistic family tree is one fun way to sum up your work. Your imagination is the only limit when it comes to this activity. Draw it, paint it, sew it, hammer it, fold

### Great Gift Idea

Artistic family trees make great gifts. Your relatives will love receiving these little pieces of history.

it, frame it, computerize it . . . anything goes! Display the finished family tree in your home for everyone to see.

Does this sound like too much work? If so, you can buy premade family tree kits from any craft store. Just fill in your family's names and dates. Add a photo of each relative and **ta-da!** You have created a suitable-for-hanging keepsake!

### It's an Art

Scrapbooking is an art! Borrow a book about this hobby from your local library. You'll find all kinds of hints and tips for making your work easier, more attractive, and more durable.

Online family tree forms are yet another easy option. With a grown-up's permission, search the web for "**family tree templates.**" You'll find all the fill-in forms you could ever want or need.

## Heritage Scrapbooks

Family trees are fun, but they're also limited. They tell only a tiny part of your family's story. For a more complete presentation, consider making a **heritage scrapbook.** These books are carefully arranged collections of photos, certificates, newspaper clippings, and other artifacts. They are a great way to display **lots** of information about your ancestors.

So what do you put into a heritage scrapbook? Anything that tells a story about your past! It's totally up to you. Here's a quick list of some typical items to get you started.

- Copies of birth, marriage, and death certificates

- Copies of other key documents

- Certificates

- Award ribbons

- Photographs

- Letters and postcards

- Maps of the family's hometown

- Memorabilia (ticket stubs, pressed flowers, etc.)

- Copy of your family tree

- Newspaper or magazine articles

- Fabric/clothing scraps

## Family Newsletters

Maybe all this family tree/ scrapbooking stuff is too artsy for your taste. You're all about the **facts, facts, facts**. If so, a family newsletter might be up your alley.

A family newsletter is just what it sounds like. It's a letter that contains news about your research findings, your family tree, your ancestor's stories, or anything else you find interesting. These publications usually come out on a regular schedule—once or twice a year, or even every month if you feel ambitious. Try writing one yourself! Send a copy to everyone who is interested in your family's unique history.

### Helpful Hint

It's easy to send family newsletters via e-mail. Keep an updated list of your subscribers' e-mail addresses. Use a computer to write your newsletter. Then send the finished file to everyone on your list in seconds!

## Websites

For the computer-savvy genealogist, a family website can be a fun way to share information. Post pictures, stories, your family tree, or anything else you like on your site. You can even blog about your research. Your relatives may love reading your online genealogical journal!

## Now What?

Websites don't have to be big or expensive. You can probably build one for **free** through your Internet service provider. Ask a grown-up to help you get started. Then invite others to visit your virtual family clubhouse.

## Meet the Family

Most genealogists talk to a bunch of long-lost relatives in the course of their research. You may have had this experience yourself. At this point, you may be thinking that some of these relatives seem pretty cool. Who knows? Maybe they would like each other. **Maybe it would be fun to get them together.**

A **family reunion** is a great way to make this happen. Family reunions are parties at which most of the guests are related. These events can be fancy or casual, big or small. It doesn't matter how you do it, as long as you invite every relative you can think of. A broader guest list is guaranteed to create a more interesting gathering!

### Helpful Hint

Post a big family tree at your reunion. Encourage your guests to fill in missing information. Many "lost" relatives have been found using this method.

If you want to plan a reunion for *your* family, here are a few things to put on the to-do list:

***Enlist an (enthusiastic) adult.*** A big party is a big deal. It takes some know-how to pull it off. Also, parties can be expensive. You'll need a grown-up's help in both of these areas.

***Focus on family history.*** It isn't just a party; it's a **reunion**. Your guests will be interested in the family's history. Do you have scrapbooks, photo albums, family trees, or other genealogy-related items to share? Are there family-themed activities your guests might enjoy? Include a few great display and event ideas in your party plans.

***Plan in advance.*** Give your guests plenty of notice, especially if they live far away. They'll need time to make travel arrangements. More advance warning equals a better turnout!

## A Growing Tradition

First family reunions tend to be small. But if you're persistent, things won't stay that way for long. Your missing relatives will hear how much fun they missed. Some of them will show up for the *next* reunion. Over time, your guest list will grow until you have a blockbuster event on your hands!

## Now What?

*Ask for information.* Reunions aren't just a chance to show off your research. They're the perfect opportunity to learn **new** things, too. Ask your guests to share their family knowledge. You might be surprised at the number of new facts you uncover.

*Have fun!* First and foremost, family reunions are about having fun. So talk, play, dance, laugh, tell stories, and enjoy each other's company. You already share a rich history with these people. It's time to make some new memories as well!

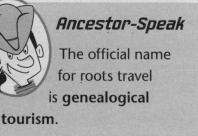

### Ancestor-Speak

The official name for roots travel is **genealogical tourism**.

## Roots Travel

When you peek into the past, you learn a lot about your ancestors' homes and communities. Are you feeling curious about these places? Are you maybe even thinking you'd like to see them yourself?

If so, go for it! **Roots travel** is a great way to bring your research to life. You can keep things simple and visit only local spots. Or you can get more ambitious and plan a long-distance trip (with a grown-up's help, of course). Either way, you're sure to learn a few fascinating things about your heritage.

Popular destinations for roots travelers include:

***Old family towns, neighbor-hoods, and homes.*** Walk your ancestors' streets, shop in their shops, and look at their homes.

***Story spots.*** Visit the places where often-repeated family stories took place.

***Graveyards.*** It can be satis-fying to visit your ancestors' final resting places. Also, you might find interesting data on your relatives' tombstones.

***Monuments with meaning.*** Did your ancestors come through Ellis Island or fight at the Alamo? Visit famous places that have special meaning to your family.

**There's the Rub**

**Grave rubbings** add a fascinating touch to any family history collection. To make a grave rubbing, tape a piece of lightweight paper over a tombstone inscription. Gently rub the paper with a thick, dark crayon. The inscription will be "copied" onto the paper. The more carefully you rub, the more detailed the grave rubbing will become!

What if you hit all the easy spots, but find that you're still hungry for more? Don't worry, genealogist. You have a whole lifetime to satisfy your craving! Someday

### Virtual Vacation

You can use Google (www.google.com) to get a bird's-eye view of almost any building, street, graveyard, or other geographic location. Use Google's map feature to find the place you need. Then click on the "Satellite" button to bring up a real photograph of the area. It's an easy way to visit your ancestors' home towns and maybe even see their houses!

you can visit hard-to-reach homesteads, foreign relatives, the "old country" where your family once lived, or other important spots. Wherever you go, you'll be following in your ancestors' footsteps . . . and this is one walk you'll never forget!

## Become a Family Historian

At this point, you have learned a lot about your family's history. But that's not all you've learned. You also have a whole new appreciation for the past, and you see that today's family documents, photos, and stories will have value someday. **You really get it, genealogist.**

So why not put your newfound knowledge to use? Become a family historian and preserve the present for future generations! It isn't hard to do. Just keep track of the types of information you were missing when you started your research. Organize it, if you can. But if you can't manage to be organized—well, that's okay. The important thing is saving the information **somehow, somewhere**, in a format that will be useful years from now. Your descendants will be grateful for your foresight.

Here are a few easy things that anyone—yes, **even a kid**—can do to preserve the family story.

*Mark milestones.* Keep a logbook of major family events such as births, deaths, and marriages. Be sure to include dates, locations, and the full spelling of all names.

*Dear diary . . .* A journal full of family stories is a gift to future generations. Take time to write down the funny or interesting things that happen in your family.

*Keep clippings.* Keep a well-organized file of newspaper and magazine clippings that concern your relatives. Include notes that explain each clipping's importance. You'll be saving your descendants untold hours of research.

*Focus on photos.* You know that bulging drawer full of family snapshots? Organize it! Do your best to put everything in chronological order. Also, write names, dates, and locations on the back of each photo. Don't you wish one of your ancestors had done this for *you*?

## Now What?

There's one more thing you can do, and it might be the most important thing of all. You could call it **saving your own life.** It's Genealogy Rule #1: **If you want to be remembered, you have to leave a trail.** So **save** those report cards and ribbons. **Keep** a journal about the things that are important to you. **Preserve** those pictures and videos. In short, go ahead and assume that everything about **you, you, you** is totally fascinating—because someday, it will be! And *that's* the biggest lesson that any genealogist can learn.

# Real Stories:
## Reunion Traditions

Many families have unique reunion traditions. These traditions let family members have fun together while building new memories and bonds.

One family holds a watery annual reunion. Relatives of all ages spend a long weekend floating down a Texas river in inner tubes. The family has enjoyed this activity for more than seventy years and has no plans to stop. "Hopefully, the reunion is like the river. It will just keep flowing," says one attendee.

Another family celebrates its history with a casual parade! Each branch of the family prepares a special banner. Groups carry their banners while marching around the parking lot of the reunion hotel. Afterward, everyone assembles for a professional photograph.

Yet another group calls their annual reunion "The Workfest." Family members spend a week each year maintaining their elderly parents' farm. They laugh, talk, and share stories while doing odd jobs. "It is truly a festive time," explains one participant.